south africa
flavours and traditions

JACANA

'We live with the hope that as she battles to remake herself, South Africa will be like a microcosm of the new world that is striving to be born.'

Nelson Mandela,
acceptance speech –
Nobel Peace Prize, 1993

4   Fishing at Kalk Bay harbour

Contents

Introduction

South Africa – a land of wide, open spaces containing an unimaginable spectrum of breathtaking landscapes that is echoed in the melange of its people, a nation known worldwide for its friendliness, humour and hospitality.

Nothing reflects the rich historical background and diverse origins of this nation better than its cuisine. Whether outside around a fire, or inside around a table, the nation's spirit is exemplified by gatherings endowed with sumptuous food, the sound of a cork popping, and much joy, laughter and storytelling.

Please join us in this remarkable celebration of life in South Africa …

Early days

Indigenous cultures have walked this subcontinent for centuries, living off the land and sea. Among those were the San and Khoi hunter-gatherers and other local groups who settled here centuries ago, foraging fresh produce from the mountain slopes and beaches, fishing the ocean waters and exploring the hinterland, experimenting with native vegetation.

It was the need for food that gave birth to the colonisation of South Africa.

Spices that we add to our food without thinking were so valuable in the fifteenth century that after the overland and Red Sea routes were closed Portuguese mariners attempted to explore the arduous sea route, hugging the African coast in less-than-adequate vessels, in order to open up a new route to the East, thus allowing the spice trade to continue. Out of this daring venture was born an age of exploration and, in 1498, Vasco da Gama pioneered the almost 10 000-kilometre sea route that opened up great possibilities for trade between the Orient and Europe. Da Gama, however, never set foot on South African soil.

It wasn't long before the Dutch also began sailing the route, and it was on one of those voyages past the Cape of Good Hope that a Dutch ship ran aground off the Cape coast. Another ship en route to Europe from the East was sent to collect the marooned passengers and on that ship was a Dutch doctor. Jan van Riebeeck treated many patients for scurvy on these voyages, and many in fact died. So when he noticed fresh water flowing from the mountain and set eyes on the fertile soil and rich marine life, it occurred to him that this scenic spot on the subcontinent would be ideal for providing the growing number of passing ships with fresh produce and water in an attempt to help save lives. And so it was that, in 1652, three Dutch ships dropped anchor in what is today known as Table Bay.

Using seeds and plant specimens he had brought with him from the Netherlands, Van Riebeeck soon established – and, despite violent storms and marauding wildlife, persisted with – a garden that would become the focus of the fledgling settlement at the Cape. And as the colony grew and, in fact, flourished, more and more people from across the globe made their way here to the southern tip of Africa, bringing with them rich cultures and an extraordinary heritage that are now the legacy of this diverse country.

And so we invite you on this journey with us through this remarkable land, with its colourful people and fascinating food. Stay a while and enjoy the tales of adventure, determination and courage at our table as we serve up this, our South Africa.

And the story continues ...

In the fledgling settlement that came to be known as Cape Town, or the Mother City as it is referred to, land was slowly given over to farmers and the colony grew. For more than 100 years the people at the Cape lived in isolation and developed their own culture, religious convictions and language, and the settlement grew both in numbers and area occupied. But the resilient farming community, not ones to let the grass grow under their feet, became restless and made the bold decision to leave the British Cape Colony and venture inland between 1835 and 1840. This proved harder than just taking a highway north, as the Cape was surrounded by mountain ranges that had yet to be conquered.

The north was unknown and believed to be teeming with 'savages', wild animals and diseases that were life-threatening. But the farmers were resourceful and filled with perseverance and hope, and after a few explorative treks, this epic adventure into the hinterland began.

Our food culture

Like most countries of the world, South Africa has borrowed recipes from the different nationalities that settled here, adapted them, in many ways enhanced them, and now call them our own.

Culinary traditions in South Africa should be seen against the backdrop of the various peoples who called this home. We inherited stories, traditions and tried-and-tested family recipes from these adventurous explorers. A fusion of indigenous cultures, the Dutch, English, French, German, Portuguese, slaves from the East, Indian workers, and the emerging Afrikaner formed the basis of our country's culinary traditions, many of which are still practised today.

23

The Strandlopers, Khoikhoi and San

Long before any European set foot in the Cape, the land was inhabited by various indigenous groups. One such group, already well established here by the time the early Dutch settlers landed, became known as the Strandlopers ('beach strollers', or nomads). The Strandlopers did not cultivate crops, nor did they own cattle, but depended entirely on nature for their food supply.

The Khoikhoi, who had settled further inland, were herders and pastoralists. They traded with other indigenous groups using mainly cattle and dagga as currency.

The San were hunter-gatherers who depended largely on game for their nourishment. Because of this, they lived in small groups, widely dispersed, and were very mobile, having long adapted to a traditional nomadic lifestyle.

These three groups were the quintessential hunter-gatherers whose intimate knowledge of and close relationship with nature afforded them a steady supply of edible indigenous plant material, some of it medicinal. In addition, their simple but effective hunting and fishing skills satisfied the need for fresh protein in their diet.

The Dutch

It was the Dutch who, on their arrival in 1652, gave birth to formal food production at the Cape. In the beginning the settlers turned to nature for their culinary needs. Plants such as wild mustard and wild sorrel were harvested. Within 14 days of landing, a vegetable garden was laid out and soon a steady supply of seeds for cultivation was arriving from abroad.

By the late 1600s, a vast array of greens could be found at the Cape, and here the practice of serving a variety of vegetables with every meal was established. The Dutch served boiled vegetables – especially cabbage, gem squash and potatoes – with a blob of butter and grated nutmeg, and this tradition continues to this day across the cultural divide.

Initially four cooks from the Dutch ships were responsible for all of the cooking within the community, and there was thus very little change in the style of the meals served here. But when farms were granted to families in 1657, the women began preparing meals of their own, each developing her own approach and cooking style. The unique character of Cape cuisine began to evolve.

In 1665, a market was started where farmers could sell their produce at fixed prices as determined by the governor. Menus were simple but the list of ingredients was growing – so much so that by the end of the seventeenth century, Governor Simon van der Stel wrote to the Dutch government of the time that the settlers lacked nothing. And, of course, the growing availability and variety of fresh produce had led to the development of a distinctive cookery style.

The custom in Holland was to prepare meat and fish with herbs and spices and that tradition continued at the Cape. Many Dutch recipes have been etched into our story, where dishes such as *frikkadels* (meatballs) are still prepared to this day and yet are virtually unknown in Holland. Pies and fruit tarts became very popular – as did pancakes – all of which are still favourites.

The Germans

German sailors in search of the opportunities in the new world arrived at the Cape in the late 1600s and many settled here as artisans and teachers. Most of the new settlers were, however, bachelors who went on to marry local women, so German culinary traditions were diluted and failed to leave an indelible mark on our cuisine. Yet the presence of a wide variety of sausages such as *boerewors* (literally translated as farmers' sausage) suggests that some influence was exerted.

Boerewors – perhaps the greatest legacy left to us by the Germans

The French

The status quo at the Cape shifted in the 1680s with the arrival of the French Huguenots, who took farming practices further inland. They arrived before the era of famous French chefs, so the style of cuisine they brought with them could best be described as homely. Farms were established in Franschhoek, or 'French corner', named for the concentration of Huguenots who settled there. Although their cooking lacked the frills we associate with classic French cuisine, it added a new dimension to local culinary history.

It was the French, too, who introduced the tradition of serving several courses at one meal. Until then, the Dutch would place the entire meal on the table at once.

Cuts of animals that did not previously feature on local tables were prepared by the French, and offal – especially tripe and trotters – became a regular delicacy.

The Huguenots were, of course, experienced farmers who contributed greatly to the improvement of viticulture and fruit production. Two local products that were influenced positively by this new location were apricots and raisins. As a result, the French left a legacy in the form of dishes such as *boerejongens* (farm boys) and *boeremeisies* (farm girls) which are, respectively, raisins and apricots preserved in brandy. Using other fruits, they made delicious *confitures* (jams), known as *konfyt* in the Afrikaans language.

The Malays

It was, however, the arrival of the first slaves in 1657 that brought about the most significant change to local cuisine. This group of people – from different parts of the world – was known collectively as 'Malay' because of a communal language, Malaya, spoken in order to understand one another. They were not, as is commonly supposed, from Malaysia.

At the time of their arrival, the Dutch controlled Indonesia, and the headquarters for the Dutch East India Company – commonly referred to as the VOC – were on the island of Java. So, unsurprisingly, the first slaves arrived from Java, and then from Madagascar. The men were generally skilled carpenters, tailors, musicians, coachmen, fishermen and plasterers, and most of the ornate gables towering above the entrances to traditional Cape Dutch homesteads were skilfully handcrafted by them.

The women were, for the most part, lace makers and experienced cooks. With them came flavours from the East and they introduced exotic Oriental dishes to the Cape kitchen using spices that they brought with them. Curries were adapted by either replacing the chillies and green ginger – important ingredients in Oriental curries – or supplementing them with local ingredients such as orange leaves, dried apricots and chutney, which were more readily available. Even today one can distinguish between traditional Oriental curries and what we call Cape Malay curries, the latter being aromatic with a hint of sweetness, combining subtle spices and dried fruit, rather than packing the

heat that characterises their Oriental counter-parts. The art of combining a variety of spices in one dish was introduced by the Malays and is still practised today.

The Malay cooks also introduced meaty curries, which went down very well with the settlers. Soon dishes such as *bobotie* (curried minced meat with raisins and other fruit and topped with a baked savoury custard), *sosaties* (kebabs) and *bredie* (stew) became favourites – and remain so in South African homes. *Sambals* were introduced, and various pickles and fruit chutneys were created too.

The wives of skilled Malay fishermen also transformed their husbands' catch into inno-vative dishes, such as pickled fish. *Bokkoms* (kippered Cape herring) became a substitute for the folk living too far north to enjoy the abundant fresh fish available at the Cape.

So great was the influence of the Malay people on our cuisine that today bobotie served with yellow rice and raisins, and malva pudding, are considered national dishes.

The Portuguese

Although the Portuguese were the first to circumnavigate this southern tip of the African continent, they never called this home. They occupied the African countries of Angola and Mozambique, where Portuguese is still spoken, but definitely added a dash of peri-peri to our food traditions. So much so that the local dried herb and spice company, Robertson Spices, bottled these flavours, like lemon, chilli, paprika and oregano, and called it 'Portuguese chicken spice'. The Portuguese community in South Africa is renowned for its knowledge of fish and seafood and, when in the mood for fish and chips, it is always a good idea to search for a Portuguese-owned outlet!

The Afrikaners

By the early to mid-1800s the Dutch, French and German immigrants had established what would essentially become a new nation – the Afrikaners. Those who ventured north were known as the *Voortrekkers* (pioneers), and during their travels developed a unique cooking culture that remains characteristic of South African culture today.

The ox and wagon and horse were the only means of transport for the Voortrekkers and provisions were limited. So, in order to survive, they had to hunt and roast the meat on open fires, thus giving birth to the *braai* (pronounced *br-eye*), or barbecue, a tradition that is now engrained in South African culture. Some ate their meat with *roosterkoek* (griddle cakes) while others, who had come into contact with indigenous black people and had been introduced to the staple food of Africa – *pap*, or mealie-meal porridge – began enjoying that with their *braaivleis*. To this day folk in the Western Cape enjoy a sandwich made from tomato, onion and

boere beskuit (farmers' rusks)

INGREDIENTS

375 ml milk
375 ml water
1½ kg butter
2½ tsp salt
5 kg cake flour, sifted
1 tbsp instant dry yeast

For the egg wash on top
2 egg yolks
100 ml milk

METHOD

• Boil the milk and the water separately.

• Melt the butter and add the boiled milk and boiling water and mix. Mix the salt into the flour and place in a large bowl. Make a hollow in the flour mixture and pour the liquid into the hollow. Mix everything together to form a bread-like dough. Knead well, cover and allow to stand in a warm, draught-free spot overnight to rise.

• Knock the dough back the next day. Grease a baking tin with butter. Form golf-ball-sized portions and pack snugly together in the bread tin. Set aside again and allow to rise to double the size in a warm spot.

• Preheat the oven to 200° C.

• Beat the ingredients for the egg wash together and lightly brush the top of the loaf. Bake until golden brown. Remove the loaf from the oven and allow to cool on a cooling rack.

• Lower the temperature of the oven to 70° C.

• Break the loaf into sausage shapes and place on a baking tray. Return to the oven, allowing the door to stand ever so slightly ajar so that the moisture escapes, and leave overnight to dry out – they should have a golden yellow colour.

• Enjoy by dunking into coffee.

cheese grilled over the coals as an accompaniment to their braai, while those living north enjoy pap. Black groups from the different regions have their own ways of preparing pap, and this has thus filtered through to others within the region.

Because there was little space for pots and pans and other cooking accoutrements on the ox wagons, the travelling settlers developed a one-pot meal called *potjiekos* (pot food). A three-legged cast-iron pot was filled with meat (mainly venison), vegetables and starch such as potatoes (when available), seasoned and covered with a lid. Hot coals were placed beneath the pot, thus creating an all-round convection heat inside.

The pot remained sealed so that the natural juices of the ingredients created a rich gravy, but the lid could be lifted to allow evaporation to reduce the gravy.

Rusks, which are similar to dried bread, and *biltong* (cured meat) were also used as sustenance on these journeys. Both would last for a long time and could be enjoyed when little else was available.

Once the Voortrekkers had settled in the central, eastern and northern parts of South Africa, they began to grow crops again and returned to many of the culinary traditions to which they had become accustomed at the Cape, but the tradition of 'on-the-move' cuisine remains to the present day.

The British

After the Napoleonic wars, Britain experienced significant unemployment, and many were encouraged to immigrate to the Cape Colony, which by the late 1700s was under British rule. On their arrival, they were given farms in the eastern reaches of the Colony, but a lack of agricultural experience meant that many eventually abandoned their farms and settled in nearby towns, some reverting to their original trades.

Some of the English did, however, stick it out on the land, with some even moving to the Natal Colony (today known as KwaZulu-Natal) where they began farming with sugar cane.

The English, of course, brought with them a new style of cooking. Although the fare was plain, venison pies and game birds were prepared. Today roast beef served with Yorkshire pudding, fish and chips, and afternoon tea are commonplace, thanks to the English.

The Indians

From the mid-1800s Indians were indentured and brought to South Africa, particularly to the Natal Colony, on contract to work as servants and as labourers in the sugar-cane plantations. Over the following five decades around 150 000 Indians were shipped over to the subcontinent, and many opted to stay on when their contracts came to an end. Today most of the Indians in KwaZulu-Natal are descendants of these migrants from colonial India. And Durban is considered the largest 'Indian' city outside of India itself.

In fact, by 1904 Indians already out-numbered the whites in Natal, and had established themselves as an important general labour force. Some worked as industrial and railway workers, while others began vegetable gardening in order to supply the local markets, and still others became fishermen.

Cuisine in India is region specific. So, because South African Indians came from diverse regions, a fusion of Indian cooking developed locally, along with a hint of influence by the Zulu people of KwaZulu-Natal. Evidence of this can be found in, for example, *chakalaka*, a classic township relish.

Classic South African Indian food has been shaped by the history of this country as a whole. According to legend, the bunny chow, a favourite in South Africa, was born in Durban through necessity during an era when the Indian Bannia class were blocked from serving Zulu customers inside their eateries.

They thus developed an edible container in the form of half a loaf of bread, hollowed out and filled this with curry. So a time-honoured tradition was born.

Contemporary influences

The passion for food, for its many ingredients and for experimentation has continued and people who visit this part of the world still enjoy lingering beside a traditional and contemporary table. Today you can pick and choose from a plethora of flavours and influences, from an endless variety of places, such as Japan, Thailand, India, France, Greece, Portugal, China, Vietnam, Turkey, Lebanon and more – all of which have influenced our journey to gourmet pleasure in some form or another.

Delights from our oceans

South Africa is situated at the meeting point of two great oceans – the Indian and Atlantic meet at Cape Agulhas, the southernmost tip of Africa.

The Atlantic Ocean is usually about 9 degrees Celsius colder than the Indian, and this temperature difference – caused by the cold Benguela current that sweeps up from the Antarctic along the west coast – promotes significant diversity in marine life. The Benguela also carries plankton, food for many fish species, which makes for great fishing. The colder waters of the Atlantic are best for rock lobster, periwinkles, black mussels, white mussels and oysters. Mussel farming is practised in places like Saldanha Bay, so unless there is a red tide, mussels are available all year round.

Off the eastern sideshore, the Mozambique (also known as the Agulhas) current, which flows south from equatorial waters in the north, brings warmer waters preferred by whales and sharks (especially great white sharks). Southern right whales arrive in Hermanus and False Bay in the Western Cape around July each year to birth their young and to breed. As a result, whale-watching has become a popular tourist attraction at various points close to the shoreline. In these warmer and safer waters, calves are birthed and helped along until they are strong enough to make the long journey back to the South Pole around November each year. Other whale species, including humpback whales, can also be seen, but the southern rights are the most common.

South Africa has exceptionally rich marine life with many species endemic to our waters. Game fish, such as snoek, tuna, dorado and yellowtail, are enjoyed regularly, as are white-fleshed fish such as hake, angelfish and kingklip. Rock lobster, *perlemoen* (abalone), periwinkles and limpets are commonplace,

but today the harvesting of lobster and abalone is strictly monitored.

Black mussels can be picked off rocks, and fish and seafood are a staple along the coastline of South Africa. Fish is generally prepared very simply, with the focus on the freshness, flavour and quality of the fish itself. Mussels are traditionally steamed, often in white wine, and served in a light creamy sauce. But many of the traditional ways of preparing fish are still widely practised, and dishes such as fish cakes, *smoorsnoek* (snoek braised with onion and tomato), pickled fish and Indian prawn curry can be found both on restaurant menus and in home kitchens. Octopus and squid are most commonly to be found along the eastern coastline, as are prawns, although most of those that make it to our table are farmed commercially.

Today our waters are monitored by SASSI (Southern African Sustainable Seafood Initiative) and consumers are informed via a comprehensive website regarding which species are plentiful and which are endangered.

River fishing

South Africa has no shortage of rivers and, as a result, freshwater fishing remains a popular pastime along the watercourse down south in the Western Cape, all the way up to Dullstroom in Mpumalanga in the north.

Rainbow trout and, to a lesser degree, brown trout, were introduced to rivers in the Eastern and Western Cape, as well as to dams in Mpumalanga, and have adapted well to local conditions. Fly-fishing has in fact become so popular that enthusiasts happily make extended trips to pursue their passion. As a result, places such as Rhodes, a tiny hamlet in the Southern Drakensberg, as well as Dullstroom in Mpumalanga have become well-known destinations. Fly-fishing has also become a popular tourist activity as the rivers are set in some of the most beautiful valleys in the world.

Up in the picturesque mountains near Franschhoek in the Western Cape, as well as in Dullstroom, trout farms produce a range of trout products for the restaurant trade, as well as for retail, including cold smoked trout, hot smoked trout and fresh trout fillets.

But fly-fishing for endemic species, such as the large-mouth yellow fish, in rivers around the country is also very popular. Many of the locals inland catch and eat freshwater species such as carp, catfish and yellow fish. If prepared correctly, these can be a treat.

Baking

Since 1659, when the Dutch governor at the Cape first granted bakers permission to practise their trade, this industry too has thrived and today, other than the large industrial bakeries that supply bread for the mass retail outlets, many artisanal bakers have stunned consumers with the ever-increasing variety of their fare. Baking at home is beginning to gain popularity once again – and there is nothing quite as satisfying and rewarding as working with bread dough, which has a life of its own.

Pies, tarts, pancakes and waffles were produced locally centuries ago, and the local culinary tradition today includes pastries that have become entrenched in our story. Most notable of these are milk tarts and pancakes (our version of a crêpe), but probably the most famous of all is the koeksister, for which the farming community and the Malays have different versions. The origin is most likely Dutch, with both the Malay slaves and Afrikaner women adding their twists to the recipe. The most common version, however, is that created by the Afrikaner farming community – the syrupy, plaited variety, as opposed to the coconut-sprinkled doughnut from the traditional Malay kitchen. A monument in Orania in the Northern Cape has even been built in honour of the koeksister and recalls a folk tradition of baking them to raise funds from which schools and churches were built.

The early *trek boere* (nomadic farmers), pastoralists and Voortrekkers found that a hollowed-out ant heap was the perfect baking oven. The Voortrekkers also used their trusted three-legged pots as baking receptacles.

It is little wonder then that baking is part of our story in this multicultural country – rural black people have their dumplings, the Malay people their rotis, Indian tandoori breads, and the hearty seed loaves that the Dutch introduced to complete the picture.

hearty seed loaf

Makes 2 loaves

METHOD

• Mix the flour, wheat bran, yeast, salt, sunflower oil and treacle sugar together, and then add the water. Mix well. The result is a runny batter rather than dough.

• Brush a bread tin lightly with butter.

• Pour the batter into the tin, and sprinkle the seeds on top. Using your fingers, gently press the seeds into the surface of the batter.

• Cover with a clean dishtowel and allow the loaf to rise in a warm, draught-free spot for 1 hour.

• While the loaf is rising, preheat the oven to 200° C.

• Once the loaf has risen, bake for 1 hour. Remove from the oven and tip the hot loaf out onto a steel rack. Allow to cool uncovered – the crust will be crunchy.

INGREDIENTS

5 cups all-purpose flour
1 cup wheat bran
2 tsp instant yeast
1 tbsp salt
2 tbsp sunflower oil
1 tbsp treacle sugar
2¾ cups warm water
melted butter (to brush the tin)
handful of seeds – linseed, pumpkin, sunflower, sesame and poppy

Preserving

The art of preserving was developed out of necessity. In the seventeenth and eighteenth centuries, housewives were forced to plan menus very carefully in order to ensure that there was never a shortage of produce to feed their families, and that whatever they had would not spoil. The hot summers at the Cape made it virtually impossible to store meat successfully and these resourceful women were forced to develop methods of preservation. This was how they began to make biltong (strips of dried and cured meat similar to jerky).

Mostly biltong is made during the winter months in what was essentially the hunting season. The lower temperatures are more suitable as they keep the meat cold and less likely to spoil.

biltong

INGREDIENTS

25 kg beef or game fillet
3 cups salt
1 cup brown sugar
1 cup coriander seeds, dry-roasted
and roughly crushed
2 tbsp white pepper
brown vinegar to sprinkle between
the layers of meat

METHOD

• Wash the meat and pat dry. Cut it into strips length-wise, about 2½ cm thick.

• Mix the salt, sugar, crushed coriander seeds and pepper, and massage the mixture into the meat. Pack the strips tightly together in layers in a couple of big dishes, and sprinkle every layer with vinegar. Allow the meat to marinate overnight.

• The next day, remove the meat from the vinegar mixture and place a hook through a thick end of the meat. Hang the strips so that they do not touch, and place in a cool, dry room with an electric fan for about 4 to 7 days, depending on humidity, temperature and personal taste.

• When dry, cut into slices and enjoy. Biltong can be kept in the freezer for a few months.

The word biltong comes from
the Dutch bil (rump) and tong (tongue or strip)

Biltong is made using the meat of a thick flank or fillet of venison or beef, from which the sinews and tendons are removed. Ostrich meat is also often used. When making biltong, keep in mind that the fresh meat will shrink by about 30 per cent during the drying process.

Smoking remains another popular way of preserving meat, especially fish, and traditional smoked snoek features prominently on menus across the country. Other traditional ways of preserving fish include salting, pickling and drying, all of which are still practised today.

The typical South African palate enjoys a combination of sweet and savoury, perhaps a result of the culinary tradition handed down to us by the Chinese who settled here during the early days of colonial settlement. Because of this, French jellies and Malay *blatjang* (fruity chutney) are often served as an accompaniment to meat dishes, especially game. Many fruits and vegetables were also preserved specifically to enjoy as an accompaniment to meat and fish dishes. Fruit was mostly sun-dried, but also often steeped in brandy.

Although fresh produce is readily available these days, preserving is an art form still practised by many. Farm kitchens generally boast rows of jars filled with preserved fruit, jams and jellies. These jars act as trophies – a testament to the cook's reputation.

Farming in South Africa

Agriculture is the foundation of developing economies such as South Africa's. And as such we have a responsibility to ensure a healthy agricultural industry that contributes to this country in many ways, especially economically, with job creation and ecotourism.

South Africa is a rich and diverse country with a varying climate and a spectacular range of vegetation and soil types. As a result, we can divide the country up into distinct farming regions where activities range from intensive crop production in winter and high summer rainfall areas, to cattle and game ranching in the bushveld, and sheep farming in the dry interior.

Only 12 per cent of the country is suitable for the production of rain-watered crops, and 69 per cent for grazing, so livestock farming is by far the largest sector. With South Africa's population growing

by about 2 per cent per annum, the 2014 population of around 53 million is projected to grow to around 82 million by the year 2035. To sustain this growth, food production must more than double in order to feed the booming nation, using the same natural resources, and this will be the challenge.

Since the 1970s, South Africa has shown interesting changes in food consumption, and as the country's middle class grows, the shift will continue. So far there has been a definite change from the staple grains consumed by the masses to a more diverse diet. An interesting development is that, according to current agricultural statistics, chicken consumption has increased in recent years by around five times what it once was, egg consumption has more or less doubled, fruit and vegetable consumption has remained constant, while red meat consumption has declined.

Agriculture is the foundation of developing economies such as South Africa's.

Fruit

Because the southern African climate ranges from subtropical through Mediterranean and continental and even to what is considered semi-desert, the country lends itself well to producing a vast spectrum of different fruits, many of which are enjoyed not only by local consumers but also throughout our large and growing export market.

South Africa is well known for the high quality of its deciduous and citrus fruit, over half of which is exported. In Mpumalanga, KwaZulu-Natal and parts of the Eastern Cape, tropical fruits such as pineapples, bananas, mangoes and papayas are grown. To celebrate pineapples in the Eastern Cape, the people of Bathurst have erected a giant pineapple as a symbol of their success in this field.

Berries

In the early 1920s, youngberries and Booysen berries were produced commercially in the Western Cape and used in the canning industry. Soon raspberries were grown as well, most of which were exported to Covent Garden in London. Slowly the industry began to develop and today an array of berries graces our supermarket shelves, the raspberry being the most popular locally.

Cherries are grown in Ceres in the Western Cape, and in Ficksburg in the Free State, while strawberries are cultivated on a large scale, especially in the Western Cape. A number of cherry and strawberry famers open their picking to the public and this has become a popular pastime during the harvesting season, with scarecrows beckoning visitors to pull up, grab a container and get picking.

Vegetables

South Africa produces a wide selection of vegetables and strives towards sustainable and organic produce. Vegetables are also grown hydroponically and in greenhouse tunnels where pests can be controlled and quality can be closely regulated.

Olives and olive oil

Olive trees thrive in our local climate, especially in the Western Cape. Despite the olive industry being a young one, our olive oils have reached the same standards as that of long-established olive oil-producing countries. Because of our latitude, we press olive oil in the European off-season, which creates considerable demand for South Africa's freshly pressed oils. International awards are abundant and we are carving a prominent place in the global olive oil industry.

Dairy

The dairy industry has developed into a huge agricultural endeavour that places a high demand on farmers to stay abreast with technology. Due to the fact that milk is perishable, there is constant pressure on the high-tech dairies that produce milk, yoghurt, cheese and other dairy products to improve on quality and quantity.

The end of the Second World War saw South Africa following the international trend of establishing small to large cooperative cheese factories that produced good-quality mass-market cheeses. Sadly this trend left little room for innovation and this controlled environment saw the marketplace flooded with commonplace varieties such as Gouda, cheddar, feta and processed cheeses, while the catering and restaurant trade laid claim to the small quantities of mozzarella and pecorino that were supplied by Italian producers.

Later, Simonsberg and Fairview – among others – began producing a more continental style of cheese. After 1986, when the industry became less regulated, a quiet revolution began to emerge in the cheese-making world and new varieties made their appearances in speciality shops. Suddenly artisanal cheese makers began flooding the market with cow, goat, water buffalo and sheep-milk cheeses – the age of artisanal cheese making was born and consumers, long deprived of this kind of creative variety, beamed with excitement.

When asked how South Africa's cheeses compare to that of the rest of the world, the proof is in the many medals that are brought home annually from various international cheese competitions.

Bees and honey

The *fynbos* (literally translated as 'fine bush') vegetation of the Western Cape, as well as the acacia trees in the Karoo, are well known for the flavour they impart to raw honey. Many small-scale beekeepers produce raw honey for the market, but honey is also produced on a large scale to satisfy the growing need.

Nuts

Although the country successfully grows pecans, walnuts, cashews, almonds, Brazil nuts and hazelnuts, we still import a lot of nuts from other countries. South Africa, however, is one of the world's most significant players in the macadamia nut industry, where the bulk is grown in the Mpumalanga and Limpopo provinces in the north of the country. Pecans and peanuts are also grown on a large scale locally. Nuts are grown for eating as well as oil production, and the demand for nuts in South Africa appears to be growing annually, largely because of the popular trend towards healthier eating.

Maize

Mieliepap or *pap* (porridge made from ground maize) is the staple food of many South Africans, and therefore the demand for maize is great.

Mieliepap is the staple food of many South Africans.

Wheat

South Africans are a bread-eating nation and the market for wheat is considerable. Whether grilling roosterkoek over coals, baking bread in outside ovens, cooking *vetkoek* ('fat cakes') in oil, or the tradition of toasting tomato-and-onion sandwiches on the braai, one will most certainly encounter bread at the table of most South Africans.

Again, artisanal bread-making is mushrooming in popularity.

Canola and sunflowers

Canola and sunflowers are grown predominantly for the production of oil. The Free State, especially, is known for the spectacular views of carpets of sunflowers, turning their heads to follow the sunlight, while canola crops flourish mainly in the Western and Southern Cape. Both these crops clothe the countryside in yellow and a visit during season, even just to take photographs, is a treat.

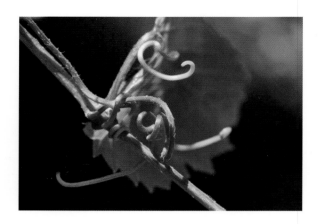

Wine grapes

Although the South African wine industry is relatively young compared with that of European countries, Cape wines are now taking their place among the best the world has to offer. Our Mediterranean climate and fertile soils, coupled with rapidly growing expertise, have set the stage for excellence.

With the arrival of the French Huguenots in the Cape in 1688 came a wine culture and skills that left an indelible impression on the local wine industry. The Huguenots, religious refugees who arrived here with very little money, had to make do with the bare minimum. As a result, established European winemaking techniques had to be adapted to local conditions.

During the 1700s and 1800s, the only great wines being produced in the southern hemisphere were the sweet wines produced at Governor Simon van der Stel's farm, Groot Constantia. In fact, during this time, these dessert wines were among the most prized dessert wines in the world, beguiling kings and emperors alike. Legend has it that Napoleon, while in exile on the island of St Helena between 1815 and 1821, asked for a glass of Constantia wine on the eve of his death. The wine was also celebrated by writers and poets, and in *Sense and Sensibility*, British novelist Jane Austen recommended to her heroine a glass of Constantia wine for its 'healing powers on a disappointed heart'.

Pinotage, South Africa's gift to the global wine industry, was first bottled in 1941. This unique cultivar was created by crossing Hermitage with Pinot Noir. Today various estates produce this unique wine, and Pinotage is enjoyed all around the world. It took a long time for Pinotage to become a world-renowned wine, but it did, winning various awards both locally and internationally.

Although many of the long-established wine farms have been handed down from generation to generation, foreign investment has recently seen overseas buyers add funding and expertise to further the local industry's insatiable quest for world-class quality and international recognition.

Most estates offer wine tours and tastings, and visitors to the Western Cape have

a choice between farms with old-world charm and those with cutting-edge technology – although these qualities often exist side by side.

Wines are also produced on a smaller scale in places such as KwaZulu-Natal and the Cape's Garden Route, but further north, in the picturesque countryside near the country's border with Namibia – where the red dust from the dry and desolate Kalahari creates the most mesmerising sunsets, and the thundering waters of the Orange River make a few final turns before heading for the Atlantic ocean – wines are also produced.

Because of the warm climate in this region, the sugar content of the grapes is much higher here, and this yields some of the country's finest dessert wines.

Grapes for brandy

The word 'brandy' comes from the Dutch word *brandewijn*, which literally means 'burnt' or 'distilled' wine.

South Africa's brandy-producing history spans three and a half centuries, and the country is the fifth-largest producer of brandy in the world today. Although the majority is consumed locally, the demand for South African brandy is growing world-wide as more and more people are exposed to it. Quality has improved dramatically, and South African brandies have fared extremely well in international competitions. With a consistent run of victories in recent years.

Brandy is South Africa's top-selling spirit drink, with average annual sales of more than 45 million litres. Its popularity seems to be due to its versatility, as it can be enjoyed neat, on ice, with various non-alcoholic mixers or in cocktails. Brandy is also widely used in our local cuisine, both modern and traditional, in dishes such as brandy tart, *Kaapsche jongens* (brandied hane-poot grapes), boerejongens (brandied raisins) and boeremeisies (brandied apricots).

One of the main cultivation areas for brandy grapes is Worcester in the Western Cape.

Hops for beer making

Beer production in South Africa has had two main influences. The first was that of the European immigrants as early as the 1650s, beginning with the Dutch, and later the English.

The second, and one that is mostly overlooked, is that of the indigenous people, who had been brewing beers made from sorghum and wheat way before the arrival of European settlers.

Today South Africa is responsible for almost half of Africa's beer consumption, and that proportion continues to grow annually. South African Breweries (SAB) is the biggest producer of local beers, and is the second largest brewery in the world, with no fewer than 20 prestigious international awards to its credit.

Perhaps because of the country's hot climate, the South African beer drinker prefers lagers to ales. An ice-cold beer in one hand and a braai tong in the other is probably the most descriptive – if not slightly caricature – way of describing South African men.

But, other than SAB, microbreweries are also popping up around the country. These enterprising initiatives are introducing South Africans to a more sophisticated and unique range of beers, and are growing in popularity – as is home-brewing, which is another exciting new trend. This initiative is supported by SAB, which often sponsors craft beer festivals around the country.

It should come as no surprise then that, although only about 40 grams of the dried product is needed to make 100 litres of beer, farming with hops is a booming industry. The industry is concentrated around the Southern Cape, which boasts some of the longest summer days in the country. Most farming is done with contracts with SAB securely in place, thus protecting them from over-production.

Other than enjoying a cold beer on a hot summer's day, locals love to prepare beer bread. Here is the recipe:

beer bread

Makes 1 loaf

METHOD

- Preheat the oven to 180° C.
- Prepare the bread tin by brushing it lightly with butter.
- Dust the tin with flour and set aside.
- Sift the flour and salt together. Stir the beer into the dry ingredients.
- Pour the mixture into the tin and bake for 45 minutes until golden brown. Remove from the oven and brush with melted butter.
- Serve with butter and preserves with a traditional braai.

INGREDIENTS

500 g self-raising flour
½ tsp salt
440 ml can beer
butter to brush tin and the loaf
flour to coat tin

Beer was brewed by the indigenous people way before the arrival of the first European settlers.

Table grapes

Table grapes for the export market are grown just inland from the wine-making heart of the Cape, where the Mediterranean climate is too cool for optimal sugar levels in the production of table grapes.

Many table grape varieties are cultivated, but the hanepoot varietal, with its distinctive muscat character, has secured a special place for itself in the hearts of South Africans. Rumour has it that Jan van Riebeeck, the first commander at the Cape, was responsible for its development. Traditionally, hanepoot was used to make *korrelkonfyt* (grape jam) and today it can be used fresh with breadcrumbs, onion and herbs as a fragrant stuffing for chicken.

Hanepoot's other claim to fame is that, in skilled hands, it yields the most luscious of dessert wines.

Sugar cane

The hub of the sugar-cane industry is KwaZulu-Natal, with some cane farming in Mpumalanga and the Eastern Cape. The aim of this industry is to supply the local market with sugar before anything is exported. Fourteen sugar mills service the cane industry.

Freshly made piping hot koeksisters are dunked into ice-cold syrup.

Medjool dates

In a quiet part of the country, near the border with Namibia, lies South Africa's best-kept secret. The farm Klein Pella is the largest producer of world-class medjool dates in the southern hemisphere, and the second largest in the world. The farm is in South Africa's Northern Cape province, with one of the harshest climates in the country; rain is scarce, with less than 10 mm falling most months, and mid-summer temperatures averaging about 38° C. These date plant-ations are irrigated with water from South Africa's largest river, the Orange River.

Livestock

South Africans eat a lot of meat – a lot! Stock farming takes place virtually across the country, where agriculture can be accommodated. The Karoo is best known for its lamb, the distinctive flavour of the meat due largely to the unique vegetation on which the animals feed. Other than sheep, stock such as cattle, pigs, ostriches and chickens are also farmed for meat production.

Game

Although big-game hunting is a draw-card today, the settlers had to learn hunting methods from the indigenous people, because hunting in Europe was reserved for the nobility.

Today, however, game farming – for both viewing and hunting purposes – is a huge industry. Visiting South Africa without experiencing a safari would mean missing out on one of the great highlights of the country.

Game meat is a healthy alternative to beef, lamb and pork because it contains very little fat. There are various ways to enjoy game, but the most popular way is in a pie. Game steaks on the braai are also popular, as are roasted legs. Game sausage, using minced game with lamb added for a little fat, is a firm favourite throughout the region.

South Africans, in general, tend to have an ethical and conservationist philosophy about hunting – 'If it won't be eaten, it should not be shot' – and this is a philosophy we encourage in our guest hunters.

Harvesting nature

The Strandlopers and Bushmen (or San people) contributed to the early menus by introducing the settlers to *veldkos* (edible wild plants) at the Cape. Thankfully, many of these plants are still known by the names they had back then. Today, more than 300 years later, there is a revival of this trend toward sourcing veldkos and local restaurants are reintroducing these ingredients to their patrons.

Waterblommetjies (pond blossoms)

These bulbs grow in still, fresh water in the Cape, and the flowers are edible. They are harvested in winter by locals wading into the water, sometimes chest-deep, to pick the flowers. These are then rinsed and can be used fresh in a stew, steamed as a vegetable, or in a soup. They can also be blanched and frozen. *Waterblommetjie bredie* (pond-blossom stew) is a traditional Cape dish.

The best months to enjoy these edible flowers are July and August when the buds are still tender and at their plumpest.

Veldkool (wild asparagus)

This plant – its Afrikaans name translates literally as 'bush cabbage' – grows in sandy soil up the West Coast. Its popular English name is derived from the fact that the tips resemble asparagus. It is only available for a short period of two to three weeks in mid-winter every year, and must be harvested before it begins to flower. It is delicious braised with onion and tomato, used in a stew, or creamed like spinach.

Suurings (wild sorrel)

Suuring stalks, rich in vitamin C, are sour and are traditionally used in a waterblommetjie bredie or in the cooking of veldkool for a little acidity, which enhances both dishes. Suurings were initially used in place of lemons, which were not available in the 1600s.

Pine nuts

With the introduction of pine trees from abroad came these wonderful edible seeds. Pine nuts are used in both sweet and savoury dishes. Traditionally they were used to make *tamme-letjie* (stick-jaw toffee).

Mushrooms

Pine ring mushrooms, which provide a creamy orange liquid when fried in butter, can be found growing in the carpet of fallen pine needles that cover mountain slopes around the Cape Peninsula.

In an attempt to produce enough wood for vat production for the growing wine industry, oaks were brought to the Cape in the late 1600s, and with them came the delights of various mushrooms from the *Boletus* family, including the cep (also known as porcini or *Boletus edulis*.)

Chicken-of-the-woods, another edible fungus, grows on oaks and eucalyptus trees. This fungus has a different mouth-feel from traditional mushrooms and is bright yellow and orange in colour. Its lemony flavour adds a delightful tang to dishes.

In KwaZulu-Natal, the *i'Khowe* is a large mushroom, meaty in texture and with an extraordinary flavour.

Kalahari truffles (*Kalaharituber pfeilii*), or desert truffles, can be found only in the Kalahari and are not part of the same family as the truffles found in Europe. They are referred to by the San people as *t'nabba* and can only be harvested in April and May – and then only when there has been good rainfall.

Foraging for mushrooms is dangerous because poisonous mushrooms can be mistaken for edible ones. Never attempt to forage without the accompaniment of someone in the know!

Wild rosemary

Not as pungent as its domestic relative, this plant occurs naturally as part of the Cape fynbos. It can be used in cooking, and its flavour is very subtle and slightly smoky.

Watercress

This plant, part of the nasturtium family, is found growing naturally beside running water. Its peppery leaves add a delicious zing to salads.

Buchu

Buchu is an indigenous herb that is often used as an infusion for tea, and has a number of medicinal properties.

Wild figs

Two species of wild fig grow on local sand dunes along the South African coast, and both these succulent plants produce edible fruit. One is the sour fig, a gelatinous fruit that is used to make a preserve that is a wonderful accompaniment to cheese.

The other is commonly referred to as the Hottentot fig, after the indigenous people who introduced the settlers to this delicacy. The fruit of this fig is sweet and can be eaten fresh.

Marula

The fruit of the marula tree – higher in vitamin C than an orange – drops from the tree just before it is ripe, and then ripens on the ground. Not only is it used in the production of South Africa's award-winning Amarula liqueur, but is enjoyed by animals and humans alike. It is great for making jams and jellies.

Peppadews

This is the trademarked brand name for sweet piquanté peppers (a cultivar of *Capisicum baccatum*) found in the Limpopo province. They have become a popular ingredient of local menus and are mostly either stuffed or pickled. They resemble cherry tomatoes and have a mild to hot flavour.

Spekboom

This succulent plant (*Portulacaria afra*) is indigenous to the Eastern Cape, where it is a flavourful snack for the local elephant population. Other than its culinary applications, this plant helps fight air pollution – it is able to capture up to four tonnes of carbon per hectare per year! It is a great addition to vegetable pickles, and can also be used in a variety of dishes, adding a slight taste of acidity to whatever you're cooking.

Madumbis

This indigenous starchy vegetable grows naturally in the eastern regions of South Africa. Its culinary applications are similar to that of a potato, although the texture is denser and the taste nuttier.

Samphire

This sea vegetable, which grows in the shallows around coastal lagoons, tastes of the ocean and is great served with fish.

Rooibos

Rooibos (meaning 'red bush' in Afrikaans) is a broomlike shrub found in fynbos regions. Although not technically a tea, this plant, with its red needle-like leaves, is used to make a herbal tea that has become one of South Africa's trademarks. It is available in red and green varieties – the red colour being the result of oxidation.

Traditionally it is enjoyed hot with a slice of lemon and honey, but iced tea and red espresso (the world's first tea espresso), made from concentrated rooibos, are fast gaining popularity.

Rooibos has many health benefits. Firstly, it contains no caffeine, and is filled with antioxidants, the most famous of which is vitamin C. Tests have shown that it also acts as an anti-inflammatory and has cardio-vascular benefits.

Mopane worms

These edible caterpillars hatch in summer. Women and children hand-pick them from mopane trees in the wild – as soon as the caterpillar has been picked it is pinched at the tail end to rupture the insides. The picker then squeezes the insides out like toothpaste and, with a flick of the wrist, discards the contents. To extend the period of enjoyment of these seasonal snacks, they are sun-dried, smoked or preserved in brine.

Mopane worms are eaten raw as a dried snack, or rehydrated and fried until crispy, or are stewed with onion, tomato and spices and served with pap. This great source of protein is enjoyed mostly in the northern parts of the country.

Outdoor cooking

South Africa's moderate climate means that outdoor cooking, ingrained in our psyche by the early indigenous people and the Voortrekkers, who learnt the art from the local populations, seems to be something of a national pastime. Folk congregate around fires, debating about whether to use wood or charcoal, each with his own way of doing things. The braai is the art of cooking meat on a metal grid over an open fire, most commonly outdoors. This popular tradition epitomises South African hospitality, and many a good laugh and meaningful conversation takes place around these fires.

Seafood, game, pork and poultry, along with the likes of vegetable kebabs, brown mushrooms and corn on the cob, end up on these grids, but the most popular of all are cuts of beef (rump, sirloin, fillet and T-bone), boerewors, chicken and lamb chops. Bread rolls (called roosterkoek) and various sosaties are also popular. The food has a smoky flavour when cooked this way outdoors.

A braai conjures up more of a mood than a meal in South African parlance. A braai is a social event shared around an open fire, and is usually handled by the men. Traditionally, it is served with salads – generally potato salad and a fresh green salad. In winter, however, when it is cold, roasted vegetables, a potato bake or pap and a *smoor* or *sheba* (tomato-and-onion sauce) may be served.

Another tradition that started very early in South Africa's history is that of making potjiekos. Preparing this stew, cooked in a round, cast-iron three-legged pot over coals, is a long process and should never be rushed. The pot is heated using small twigs or just a few coals at a time, just keeping the contents simmering. The potjie involves mostly lamb, chicken or game meat and lots of vegetables – and is usually served with rice.

These outdoor get-togethers are casual and everyone helps themselves. Guests sit around the fire and eat from plates on their laps, or around an informally laid table.

Weather to go

South Africa's climate is as diverse as its people. The country is situated in the southern hemisphere's sub-tropical zone, and has a greater variety of climates than most other countries in sub-Saharan Africa. It also has lower average temperatures than other countries within this range of latitude, because much of the interior of South Africa is at a higher elevation.

Typical of the southern hemisphere, the coldest days are in June, July and August. On the central plateau, because of the higher altitude, temperatures often drop to below zero during winter. The coastal regions, especially the east coast, are warmer in winter than the inland regions.

South Africa is a sunny country, with rainfall averaging 450 mm, compared to the global average of 860 mm. Rainfall is greatest in the east and decreases gradually westward, with semi-desert areas occuring along the western part. For the largest part, rain falls mainly in summer, and comes in the form of brief afternoon thunderstorms. The Western Cape is an exception as it boasts a Mediterranean climate, with rain during the winter months.

In winter snow collects on the high mountains in and around the Cape, and also on the mountain peaks of the Drakensberg (from the Afrikaans *draak* for 'dragon', and *berg* for 'mountain'), which winds through a large part of the country.

The summer months extend from December to February and winter from June through to August.

Some interesting facts

● South Africa comprises 1 221 037 square kilometres, which means that almost two Frances, about three and a half Germanies, and more than nine Englands would fit into the land area of South Africa.

● According to the *Guinness Book of World Records*, South Africa has the most official languages of any country in the world: English, Afrikaans, isiZulu, isiXhosa, Sesotho, Setswana, Sepedi, Xitsonga, siSwati, isiNdebele and Tshivenda.

● There are nine provinces and the country borders onto Namibia, Botswana, Zimbabwe, Mozambique, Swaziland and Lesotho.

● Cape Town's Table Mountain is believed to be one of the oldest mountains in the world and one of the planet's 12 main energy centres, radiating magnetic, electric and spiritual energy.

● The world is divided into six floral kingdoms, all of which encompass several countries and sometimes continents. The Cape Floral Kingdom, however, is both the smallest and the richest, with 9600 plant species, 70% of which are indigenous to a small area in the Western Cape. Table Mountain is home to about 1500 of these species, more than can be found in the entire United Kingdom.

● South Africa is the second largest exporter of fruit in the world.

● We also have the longest wine route in the world, and the oldest wine industry outside of Europe and the Mediterranean.

● The Kruger National Park supports the greatest variety of wildlife species on the

- The Palace of the Lost City resort hotel is the largest theme resort hotel in the world as well as the largest building project undertaken in the southern hemisphere. Surrounding the Palace is a 25-hectare manmade botanical jungle with almost two million plants, trees and shrubs.

- The Blyde River Canyon is the third largest canyon in the world, and the largest green one. The Grand Canyon in the United States and the Fish River Canyon in Namibia are the first and second largest, but both are very dry.

- South Africa is home to the world's smallest and largest succulent plants – the smallest measures less than 1 cm and the largest is the baobab tree.

- Kimberley has the biggest manmade hole in the world.

- Vilakazi Street in Soweto in Gauteng is the only street in the world to have housed two Nobel Peace Prize winners: Nelson Mandela and Archbishop Emeritus Desmond Tutu.

- This country is the world's largest producer of macadamia nuts.

- The world's oldest meteor scar can be found in Parys in the Free State and is called the Vredefort Dome. It is a UNESCO World Heritage Site.

- With two oceans, the country's topography and its prevailing winds, South Africa boasts a natural environment that has everything from deserts, mountains, escarpments, plateaus, savannah grasslands and bushveld to wetlands and lush subtropical forests.

- Dr Christiaan Barnard performed the first human heart transplant in the world at Groote Schuur Hospital in Cape Town in 1967. He was also the first to do a 'piggy-back' transplant in 1971, and the first to do a heart-lung transplant.

● Most of the world's proto-mammalian fossils are found in the Karoo region. This region is home to some of the best fossils of early dinosaurs.

● The world's largest diamond is the Cullinan Diamond, found in South Africa in 1905. It weighed 3 106.75 carats uncut. It was cut into the Great Star of Africa (530.2 carats), the Lesser Star of Africa (317.40 carats) and 104 other diamonds of nearly flawless colour and clarity. Some of these now form part of the British crown jewels.

- Three of the world's five fastest land animals are to be found in South Africa: the cheetah, which tops the list at just over 100 kilometres per hour, the blue wildebeest, and the lion.

- The oldest remains of modern humans were found in Klasies River Cave in the Eastern Cape. They are well over 100 000 years old.

- In the eastern part of South Africa, scientists have found traces of blue-green algae dating back 3500 million years. This is some of the earliest evidence of life on Earth.

- There are more than 2000 shipwrecks, dating back at least 500 years, off the South African coast. In addition, several ships, including the *Waratah*, simply vanished without a trace along the southern coastline.

- Approximately 900 bird species are found in South Africa alone, which represents 10% of the world's total bird species.

- South Africa is the first, and to date the only, country to build nuclear weapons and then voluntarily dismantle its entire nuclear weapons programme.

- South Africa has the second oldest film industry in the world. Only the USA created a film industry before South Africa. In 1898 The Empire Palace of Varieties in Commissioner Street, Johannesburg, first screened films of views of Johannesburg taken from the front of a tram and of the President of the Transvaal Republic, Paul Kruger, leaving his house for the Raadsaal. Today the favourable exchange rate, good weather conditions, varied locations and world-class production facilities have made South Africa a preferred destination for international film, television and commercial producers.

- South African brewery SABMiller ranks, by volume, as the largest brewing company in the world.

South Africa today

South African cuisine remains a fusion of styles and flavours of the various cultures that call this home – a Rainbow Nation indeed.

Despite representing one of the world's youngest democracies, thanks to great men and women over the centuries, the country has triumphed and remains a sought-after tourist destination. Like our national anthem, this country is a coming together of many nations and cultures.

Nkosi sikelel' iAfrika
Maluphakanyisw' uphondo lwayo,

Xhosa: God bless Africa.
Let Africa's horn be raised,

Yizwa imithandazo yethu,
Nkosi sikelela, thina lusapho lwayo.

Zulu: Listen to our prayers,
Lord, bless us, we are the family of Africa.

Morena boloka setjhaba sa heso,
O fedise dintwa le matshwenyeho,
O se boloke, O se boloke setjhaba sa heso,
Setjhaba sa, South Afrika – South Afrika.

Sesotho: Lord, bless our nation,
Stop wars and suffering,
Save it, save our nation,
The nation of South Africa – South Afrika.

Uit die blou van onse hemel,
Uit die diepte van ons see,
Oor ons ewige gebergtes,
Waar die kranse antwoord gee,

Afrikaans: Out of the blue of our heavens,
From the depth of our sea,
Over our everlasting mountains,
Where the cliffs give answer …

Sounds the call to come together,
And united we shall stand,
Let us live and strive for freedom
In South Africa our land.

English

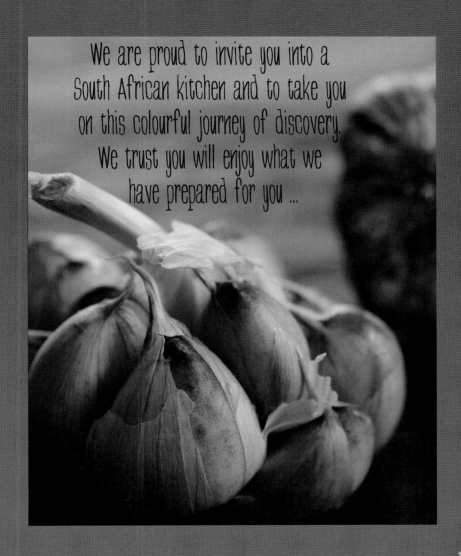

We are proud to invite you into a
South African kitchen and to take you
on this colourful journey of discovery.
We trust you will enjoy what we
have prepared for you ...

recipes

Amarula malva pudding

INGREDIENTS
1 egg
1 cup sugar
1 tbsp smooth apricot jam
1 cup flour
1 tsp bicarbonate of soda
generous pinch of salt
½ cup milk
½ cup cream
1 tbsp butter
1 tsp white vinegar

Sauce
¼ cup milk
¼ cup cream
100 g butter
½ cup sugar
¼ cup hot water
¼ cup Amarula liqueur

METHOD
• Preheat the oven to 180° C.
• Beat the egg, sugar and jam together on high for about 15 minutes. While beating, sift the flour, bicarbonate of soda and salt into a bowl. After 15 minutes, add ½ cup milk and ½ cup cream to egg mixture, alternating with the flour mixture.
• Melt the butter, add the vinegar and add to the mixture. Combine well.
• Pour into a dish, approximately 20 cm in diameter, and bake for 45 minutes to 1 hour until rich brown in colour.
• For the sauce, melt together ¼ cup milk, ¼ cup cream, the butter, ½ cup sugar, and hot water so that it is ready when the pudding comes out the oven. While warm, remove from the heat and stir the Amarula liqueur into the mixture.
• Pour the sauce over the pudding as it comes out the oven, and cover with foil again until ready to serve. The hot pudding absorbs the hot sauce and the texture becomes soft and spongy.
• Serve warm with fresh berries and custard.

Amarula liqueur is a cream-based drink made from the fruit of the marula tree, a favourite of elephants. It can be substituted with a similar liqueur.

'Malva' is the Afrikaans word

'or marshmallow, which refers to the texture of this dish.

beer-battered hake

Serves 8

METHOD

• Place the flour in a bowl and add the beaten egg. Combine and gradually whisk the beer into the mixture to form a smooth batter. Season with salt and pepper. Cover and place in the refrigerator to rest.

• Heat the oil in a saucepan – about 8 cm deep – until hot. To test if it is hot enough, drop a teaspoonful of the batter in the oil – it should bubble immediately. Pat the fish fillets dry and dip one fillet at a time into the batter to coat, and from there, straight into the oil.

• Deep-fry for 3 to 4 minutes until golden and cooked through. Drain the fish on paper towel and serve immediately with lemon wedges and tartar sauce.

• For the tartar sauce, gently mix together the chopped gherkins, capers, chives and parsley, adding the tarragon, lemon juice and zest, as well as the mayonnaise. Cover and keep cold for 1 hour before using.

INGREDIENTS

225 g self-raising flour
1 large egg, lightly beaten
375 ml chilled beer
salt and pepper to season
vegetable oil for deep-frying
8 x 120 g hake fillets
lemon wedges to serve

Tartar sauce

½ tbsp each of chopped gherkins, capers, chives and parsley
3 generous pinches of finely chopped French tarragon
juice and finely grated zest of a small lemon
½ cup of good, rich mayonnaise

When the fish is cooked, the flesh will be white and flaky.

biltong pâté

Serves 4

INGREDIENTS
75 g biltong powder
100 g smooth cream cheese
25 g Gorgonzola
125 ml cream
1 ml ground coriander

METHOD
• Place all the ingredients in a bowl and combine.
• Serve with brown seed loaf, Melba toast, or water biscuits as part of a snack platter.

The pâté tends to thicken when left, so add more cream for a softer consistency.

Serves 6

METHOD

• Preheat the oven to 180° C.

• Heat the olive oil in a saucepan and fry the onions until transparent. Add the garlic and cook through. Sprinkle the curry powder over the onions and add the salt. Cook on a low heat to allow the flavour of the curry to be released.

• Add the mince and stir until the meat is cooked and any lumps have disintegrated. Then add the vinegar and cook together for about 15 minutes. Add the turmeric and stir through.

• Soak the bread in the milk for a few minutes. Remove the soggy bread, squeeze lightly and mash with a fork. Add the bread to the meat mixture and then add the eggs. Stir with a wooden spoon.

• Add the apricot jam, raisins and grated apple to the meat and stir into the mixture. Set aside to cool.

• When the mixture has cooled, form balls of about the size of a golf ball. Roll in the flour and set aside.

• Heat a drizzle of the olive oil in the bottom of a pan. When hot, fry the meatballs briefly until they brown slightly on all sides.

• Serve with chutney on basmati rice with seasonal vegetables or a green salad.

INGREDIENTS

2 tbsp olive oil (plus a little for frying)
2 onions, peeled and sliced
2 cloves garlic, peeled and chopped
2 tbsp curry powder, medium strength
1½ tsp salt
1 kg minced lamb
1 tbsp vinegar
2 tbsp turmeric
2 thick slices white bread, crusts removed
1 cup milk (to soak the bread)
3 eggs, lightly beaten
2 tbsp smooth apricot jam
1 cup seedless raisins
1 Granny Smith apple, peeled and grated
flour (to roll balls in)

boerewors rolls

Makes 4 rolls

INGREDIENTS

2 tsp butter
1 onion, peeled and sliced
2 tsp treacle sugar
1 tsp wholegrain mustard
3 tbsp olive oil
450 g boerewors
4 hotdog rolls

METHOD

• Melt the butter and fry the onion slices until they begin to brown. Lower the heat and add the sugar, stirring until the sugar has dissolved. Add the mustard and set aside.

• Heat the olive oil in a pan. Cut the boerewors into sections of about 15 cm long and fry until brown on both sides.

• Cut a slit along each hotdog roll. Place a sausage inside the slit and top with the caramelised onion.

• Serve with chakalaka (see page 127).

Boerewors done on the braai will have a wonderful smoky flavour complemented by the sweetness of the caramelised onions.

bunny chow with vegetable curry

INGREDIENTS

2 tbsp olive oil

1 onion, peeled and chopped

2 cloves garlic, crushed

4 curry leaves

2 tsp curry powder

1 tomato, peeled and cubed

125 ml water

100 g butternut, peeled and diced

3 medium-sized carrots, peeled and cut into small chunks

180 g green beans, topped and tailed and cut into thirds

2 large potatoes, peeled and cubed

METHOD

• Heat the oil in a saucepan and fry the onion until trans-parent. Add the garlic and fry again briefly, taking care not to allow the garlic to turn brown.

• Add the curry leaves and curry powder and fry to release its flavour before adding the tomato. Cook on a very low heat for 5 minutes.

• Turn the heat up to medium and add the water and vegetables. Allow to simmer slowly until all the vegetables are tender.

• To serve, cut a loaf of white bread into thirds. Using only the two outer pieces, hollow out the soft bread and place the curry into the hollow. Press some of the chunks you removed from the centre of the loaf back into the hollow, covering the curry, and serve.

Depending on personal preference, mild, medium or hot curry powder can be used.

Bunny chows are best eaten by hand.

South African brandies are world class.

Cape brandy pudding

Serves 6 to 8

METHOD

- Preheat the oven to 180° C.
- To make the tart, sprinkle the bicarbonate of soda over the dates and add the boiling water. Set aside to cool.
- Cream the butter and sugar together. Add the egg and beat well. Add the date mixture to the butter mixture and mix.
- Sift the dry ingredients – cake flour, baking powder and salt – together and add to the butter mixture. Add the nuts and orange zest, mix well and spoon into a well-greased pie dish.
- Bake for 45 minutes to 1 hour.
- While the pudding is baking, prepare the syrup by heating butter, sugar and water in a small saucepan and stir until the sugar dissolves. Add the vanilla essence and a pinch of salt and turn up the heat to bring the mixture to the boil. Boil for 5 minutes.
- Remove the mixture from the stove and stir in the brandy. When the pudding is baked, remove it from the oven and pour the syrup over the hot pudding.
- Serve the pudding hot as dessert, with a scoop of ice cream, or cold as a tart with thick cream.

INGREDIENTS

Tart
1 tsp bicarbonate of soda
250 g stoned dates, chopped
250 ml boiling water
60 g butter
1 cup sugar
1 large egg
1½ cups cake flour
heaped ½ tsp baking powder
heaped ½ tsp salt
½ cup chopped walnuts and pecan nuts
zest of 1 orange

Syrup
1 tbsp butter
1¼ cups sugar
250 ml cup water
1 tsp vanilla essence
pinch of salt
100 ml brandy

chakalaka

Makes 1 litre

METHOD

• Heat the oil in a large pot. Fry the onion until it just begins to turn brown. Add the spices – curry powder, paprika and turmeric – and cook for two minutes for the flavours to be released.

• Add the remainder of the ingredients, toss to mix and cook over a medium heat for 10 minutes.

• Spoon the hot mixture into sterilised jars and seal tight.

• Serve with a boerewors roll (see page 120).

INGREDIENTS

3 tbsp oil (for frying)
1 onion, finely chopped
1 tbsp curry powder
1 tsp paprika
½ tsp turmeric
5 large carrots, peeled and roughly grated
1 cup green beans, chopped
4 tomatoes, peeled and chopped
50 g fresh ginger, peeled and grated
2 green chillies, chopped
2 cloves garlic, peeled and crushed
4 fresh curry leaves
1 tbsp lemon juice, freshly squeezed
2 tbsp sugar
70 g tomato paste
2 tsp vegetable stock powder
3 cups very finely grated cabbage
1 cup baked beans
1 tsp parsley, roughly chopped
1 tbsp vinegar
salt and freshly milled pepper to taste

cherry tomato jam

INGREDIENTS
2 cups cherry tomatoes, halved
crossways
160 g sugar

METHOD
• Macerate the tomatoes with the sugar for about 60 minutes until the sugar is dissolved.
• Bring to the boil over medium heat, before reducing the heat to a simmer. Reduce the liquid until left with about ¾ of the original volume. To test whether the jam is ready, drop a small amount onto a cold saucer, if it remains separated when a finger is pulled through the jam, it is ready.
• Skim any foam which may have formed off the top before spooning the jam into a 250 ml sterilised jar.
Serve with beer bread (see page 81).

Sweet and tangy

chicken pie

Serves 6

METHOD

• Preheat the oven to 180° C.

• Heat the oil in a heavy-bottomed pot and fry the onion until soft and transparent. Add the chicken, stock, bay leaves, cloves, coriander, potatoes and carrots, and cook covered over a medium to low heat for 45 minutes.

• Remove lid and reduce the juices until the pot is moist – in other words, not dry but not swimming in liquid either. Remove the chicken pieces, debone and cut into bite-sized pieces. Set the gravy aside.

• Whisk the egg yolk, lemon juice, brandy and cream together and add to the gravy in the pot. Add the parsley and the chicken and mix well. Spoon the mixture into a greased baking dish of about 28 x 20 cm.

• To make the pie crust, cut one sheet of cold puff pastry into strips of 4 cm wide lengthways. Cut the other into strips of 4 cm breadthways. On a sheet of plastic, place the longer strips alongside one another and then plait the shorter strips through to form a weave pattern. Carefully cover the pie with the puff pastry, secure the edges and trim off all excess pastry. Brush with the beaten egg.

• Bake for 45 minutes until puffed up and golden brown in colour.

• Serve with seasonal vegetables.

INGREDIENTS

4 tbsp olive oil
1 large onion, thinly sliced
1½ kg chicken thighs
1 litre chicken stock
2 bay leaves
¼ tsp ground cloves
¼ tsp ground coriander
2 medium potatoes, peeled and diced
4 medium carrots, peeled and diced
1 egg yolk
juice of 1 lemon
1 tbsp brandy
2 tbsp cream
2 tbsp chopped parsley
2 sheets ready-made puff pastry
1 egg, lightly beaten

coffee and turmeric leg of lamb

Serves 6 to 8

METHOD

- Preheat the oven to 180° C.
- Mix the coffee, coriander and turmeric together and rub the mixture into the leg of lamb. Drizzle with a little olive oil and place in a roasting pan. Season with salt and pepper and add the cardamom pods.
- Cover with foil and place in the preheated oven. After 2 hours, remove the foil and return to the oven for 1 hour. Remove from the oven and allow to rest for 20 minutes before carving.

INGREDIENTS

1 tbsp coffee, freshly ground
1½ tsp ground coriander
2 tsp turmeric
1.5 kg leg of lamb
olive oil
black pepper, freshly milled
salt to season
5 cardamom pods

Mutton is better than lamb. It needs to cook for longer, but the longer cooking process enhances the effect of this exquisite combination of flavours.

corn-and-cheese samoosas

Makes 36

INGREDIENTS

410 g can of whole-kernel corn, drained
200 g mild cheddar, finely grated
36 sheets *pur* pastry
sunflower oil (for deep-frying)
water

METHOD

• Mix the corn and cheese and set aside.

• Cover the pastry with a damp cloth. Fold each rectangle into a triangular parcel as illustrated. Fill the parcel with the corn and cheddar mix and complete the folding process. Seal the final side using a moistened finger. Keep each filled parcel under a damp cloth to prevent the pastry from drying out.

• In a deep saucepan, heat the oil until hot. Test the heat by dropping a small piece of pastry into it – the pastry should bubble. Fry the parcels until golden brown on both sides.

• Remove and drain on paper towel. Serve immediately, 3 per person, as a starter or a snack with drinks.

Pur is ready-made samoosa pastry. It is widely used in Indian cuisine as well as Cape Malay dishes. It can be substituted with phyllo pastry, brushed with butter and baked, rather than deep-fried.

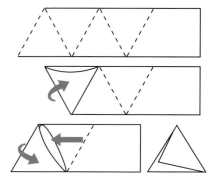

date balls

Serves 6

INGREDIENTS
115 g butter, cubed
100 g sugar
2 tsp instant coffee
250 g dates, pips removed and chopped
200 g Marie biscuits, broken into small pieces
5 ml vanilla essence
50 g fine coconut

METHOD
• Place the butter and sugar in a pot and warm over low heat until the sugar has dissolved. Add the coffee granules and stir until dissolved.

• Add the dates and cook until the dates have disintegrated, stirring occasionally. Add the biscuits and vanilla essence and mix well.

• Using a tablespoon measure for size, form balls and roll those in the coconut. Repeat until mixture has been used up.

• Store in an airtight container.

deep-fried stuffed pap balls

Serves 10

INGREDIENTS

Pap
100 g pap
500 ml water
½ tsp salt
25 g butter

Meatballs
250 g lean lamb mince
½ onion, peeled and very finely chopped
1 tsp salt
freshly milled black pepper to taste
¼ tsp ground nutmeg
2 tbsp chives, finely chopped
1 tbsp flat-leaf parsley, finely chopped
1 medium egg, beaten
2 tbsp olive oil

METHOD

• Place the pap in a heavy-based saucepan. Add water and salt. Gently bring to the boil, stirring constantly to prevent lumps from forming. Reduce the heat and allow to bubble gently, stirring occasionally, for 20 to 30 minutes. Stir in the butter and then set aside to cool.

• To make the meatballs, mix together the minced lamb, the finely chopped onion, nutmeg, chives, parsley, salt and black pepper. Add half of the beaten egg to bind the mixture and set the other half aside for later. Roll small meatballs of about 1½ to 2 cm in diameter – this mixture makes about 30 meatballs. Drizzle 2 tbsp oil into the bottom of a small pan and cook the meatballs on a medium heat until browned on both sides (7 to10 minutes.) Set aside to cool.

INGREDIENTS *continued*

Tomato sauce

3 tbsp olive oil

2 medium-sized onions, chopped

2 large cloves garlic, crushed

400 g can peeled-and-chopped tomato

1 tbsp oregano, chopped

1 tsp salt

pepper to taste

1 tsp sugar

To roll the pap arancini in

200 g breadcrumbs

vegetable oil to deep-fry

METHOD *continued*

• For the sauce, heat 3 tbsp olive oil in a saucepan and fry the 2 roughly chopped onions until they begin to brown. Lower the heat, add the garlic and fry briefly, making sure the flavour is released without the garlic burning. Add the chopped tomato, oregano, salt and pepper, and allow to gently simmer for 20 minutes before adding the sugar. Remove from the heat and set aside.

• When the mixture has cooled, roll a ball of about the size of a walnut. Press a hole in the middle using your thumb, and place the meatball inside. Press the pap around it to enclose it, and roll into a neat ball again. Dip into the other half of the beaten egg mixture and roll in the breadcrumbs. Leave to set for 10 minutes before deep-frying in hot oil until golden brown.

• Heat the sauce and serve topped with the sauce as a starter.

These are inspired by Sicilian arancini, Italian for 'little oranges'.

dried fruit and spekboom pickle

Makes 2 cups

METHOD

• Pour boiling water over the dried fruit and leave to soak for 30 minutes. Drain and slice the bigger pieces into strips and place in a large bowl.

• Pour the vinegar into a cup and stir in the mustard seeds and harissa blend. Pour this over the fruit in the bowl. Then add all the remaining ingredients and mix well. Store in a sterilised jar. Allow to stand for at least 3 days before serving.

INGREDIENTS

250 g mixed dried fruit
125 g dried cranberries
½ cup brown vinegar
1½ tsp black mustard seeds
½ tsp harissa blend of spices
¼ cup sunflower oil
1 tsp turmeric
1 tsp salt
1 tsp fresh garlic, crushed
¼ cup spekboom leaves
3 tbsp sugar
2 sticks cinnamon
3 tbsp golden syrup

'Portulacaria afra', or 'spekboom' in Afrikaans, is an edible succulent plant which adds an acidic tang to this pickle.

fish biryani

INGREDIENTS

50 ml oil
1 large onion, peeled and sliced
4 cardamom seeds
2 sticks cinnamon
5 ml fresh ginger, peeled and finely chopped
4 cloves garlic, peeled and crushed
5 ml fennel powder (*barishap*)
5 ml cumin seeds (*jeera*)
5 ml ground coriander
15 ml leaf masala
100 ml water
1 kg fish, cubed
salt to season
6 small potatoes, peeled and cubed
½ cup tomatoes, peeled, pips removed and chopped
250 ml vegetable stock (plus a little extra if needed)
200 g uncooked basmati rice
salted water (to cook the rice)
5 ml turmeric
125 ml dry brown lentils (*masoor*), generously covered in water
½ cup almond slivers
¼ cup sultanas
4 hardboiled eggs, quartered

METHOD

• Heat the oil in a saucepan and fry the onion, cardamom, cinnamon, ginger and garlic until onion is tender. Add the fennel powder, cumin seeds, coriander, leaf masala and 100 ml water. Simmer until the mixtures forms an aromatic paste.

• Season the fish with salt and add together with potatoes to the paste, frying until the mixture takes on a rich yellow colour. Add the chopped tomatoes and vegetable stock, and cover and braise until the potatoes are soft. Add a little extra stock if the dish seems too dry.

• Place the rice in a pot and cover with salted water to about 2 cm above the surface of the rice. Add the turmeric and bring to the boil. Lower the heat and allow the rice to almost steam until tender and the water has cooked away. Remove from the heat and, using a fork, separate the grains until fluffy. Place the lid back on and set aside.

• Cook the lentils in water until soft. Make sure that they remain covered with water. When soft, remove from the heat, drain and set aside.

• Combine the rice and lentils with the almonds and the sultanas, and arrange layers of the mixture and rice in a saucepan. Add ¼ cup boiling water. Cover with waxed paper, followed by the lid and steam on a very low heat for 30 minutes.

• To serve, dish onto a serving platter. Place the quartered eggs on top just before serving.

game-and-lamb pie

Serves 12

METHOD

• Heat the oil in a pot and fry the onion until it starts to brown. Add the game meat and the lamb knuckles and allow to brown a little. Add the carrots, pour over the ver-juice and season with salt and pepper. Cover with a lid.

• As soon as the contents are bubbling, turn the heat down and allow to bubble for 1 hour or until the meat is very tender.

• Use a slotted spoon to remove the meat from the pot. Thicken the juices in the pot with gravy thickener. Remove all the bones from the lamb knuckles and mix enough gravy into the meat to ensure that it is all moist. Set the mixture aside.

Preheat the oven to 180° C.

• To make the crust, place the flour in a bowl. Use your fingertips to rub the butter into the flour until it resembles breadcrumbs. Add the egg yolks, salt and milk and then mix. In a separate bowl, beat the egg whites to stiff and fold them into the pastry.

• Spoon the meaty filling into a bowl and spoon the crust onto it in big spoonfuls. Try to cover most of the meat with the pastry.

• Place in the oven and bake until golden brown and the juices are bubbling.

• Serve with a side salad or seasonal vegetables.

INGREDIENTS

Filling
4 tbsp olive oil
1 large onion, peeled and sliced
1 deboned leg of springbok, sinews removed and cut into big chunks
1 kg lamb knuckles
8 medium-sized carrots, peeled and cut into chunks
2 cups verjuice
salt and freshly milled black pepper to season
gravy thickener

Crust
1½ cups self-raising flour
125 g butter, cold
2 eggs, separated
½ tsp salt
125 ml milk

gluten-free spicy maize muffins

Makes 6 large muffins

METHOD

• Preheat the oven to 180° C.

• Mix 250 ml of the cold milk with the pap and set aside. Heat the remaining 250 ml milk, and add the pap mixture, salt, sugar, vanilla essence and butter to the hot milk and simmer for a few minutes. Allow to cool slightly.

• Beat the eggs well. Stir the pap mixture into the eggs and add the fruit, nuts and spices. Stir in the baking powder. Spoon the mixture into a well-greased muffin tray. Bake in the preheated oven for 30 minutes until golden brown.

• Serve with butter and preserves.

INGREDIENTS

300 g pap (maize)
500 ml milk
½ tsp salt
2 tbsp yellow sugar
1 tsp vanilla essence
50 g butter
3 eggs
100 g mixed citrus peel
50 g sun-dried crimson raisins
handful pistachios, shelled
1 tsp cinnamon
1 tsp mixed spice
2 tsp baking powder

Spicy and a healthy alternative

ginger preserve

INGREDIENTS
125 g fresh, young ginger roots
250 g white sugar
1 cup water
2 tsp liquid glucose

METHOD
• Clean and peel the ginger roots using the edge of a spoon to scrape off the papery skin with-out cutting into the flesh. Cut the roots into thumb-sized lengths and soak overnight in enough cold water to cover them.
• The next day, drain the ginger and place in a stockpot with enough water to generously cover the ginger and bring to a boil. Then drain, and repeat the boiling process with fresh water three times, or until ginger is tender. Older roots may require extra boiling time.
• Make the syrup by placing the sugar in a pot with ¼ cup water, and gently heat over a low heat, stirring until all the sugar has dissolved. Take care not to bring the mixture to the boil until all the sugar has dissolved.
• When the sugar has dissolved, turn the heat to high, cover the pot with the lid and allow to simmer vigorously for 2 minutes. Remove the lid and stir gently while simmering until the syrup turns deep amber. Remove from the heat immediately.
• With extra care, add the remaining ¾ cup water, a little at a time. When the bubbling settles, stir gently to mix. Add the ginger and bring to the boil for another 10 to 12 minutes until the syrup has thickened slightly. Then add the liquid glucose to prevent crystallisation.
• Sterilise two 250 ml jars by immersing them in a pot of water and boiling them, together with the lids, for 10 minutes. Spoon the hot ginger and syrup into the jars and seal. Set aside and allow to stand overnight at room temperature. Allowing the ginger to soak in the sugar syrup at room temperature allows the sugar to permeate the ginger, preserving and sweetening it; this also allows the flavour of the ginger to permeate the syrup.
• Serve as part of a cheese platter.

The ginger can be kept in the sterilised jars for up to a year.

green-bean bredie

Serves 6

INGREDIENTS

3 tbsp olive oil
1 large onion, peeled and sliced
1 kg lamb neck, cut into portions
250 ml water (more if needed)
350 g green beans, topped and tailed
6 medium-sized potatoes
salt and white pepper to taste

METHOD

• Heat the oil in a heavy-bottomed pot and fry the onion until transparent. Add the meat and brown along with the onions. Pour the water over the meat and cover with a lid. Allow to braise at a very low simmer for 40 minutes, making sure the liquid does not cook dry.

• Cut the green beans into thirds, and peel and cut the potatoes in half lengthways. Add the potatoes to the meat first and then top with the beans. Season with salt and pepper. At this point you might need to add some liquid, 125 ml at a time.

• Cook for about another 30 minutes or until the potatoes are tender.

• Serve on a bed of basmati rice.

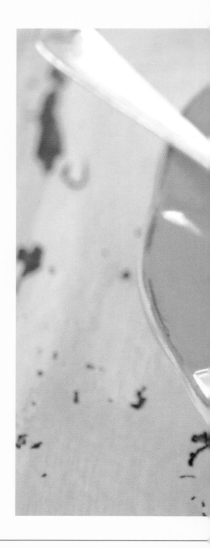

jaffels with savoury mince

Serves 6

METHOD

• Heat the olive oil in a saucepan and fry the onion until transparent. Add the mince and cook, using a fork to ensure that the meat does not clump together. Add the salt and all the spices and mix these into the meat. Allow to cook until the liquids have just been absorbed and then add the chutney. Mix and set aside.

• On the side of the bread slice that is not buttered, spread a layer of mustard, topped with a layer of mince, then a layer of cheese and lastly a slice or two of tomato. Season with salt and pepper.

• Heat the jaffel pan on both sides on a gas flame. When it is hot on both sides, place the sandwich inside and clip closed to secure. Place the iron back on the gas flame on a moderate heat.

INGREDIENTS

3 tbsp olive oil
1 onion, peeled and finely chopped
750 g minced lean lamb
1 tsp salt
¼ tsp ground coriander
¼ tsp ground cumin
¼ tsp ground paprika
4 tbsp fruity chutney
12 slices white bread, buttered one side only
cheddar cheese, grated
Dijon mustard
ripe tomatoes, sliced
salt and pepper to season

The white bread can be substituted with brown or wholewheat.

A great idea for fireside mealtimes

koeksisters

INGREDIENTS

Syrup

1 kg sugar
500 ml water
2 pieces of fresh ginger
2 ml cream of tartar
juice of ½ a lemon
pinch salt

Dough

240 g cake flour
4 tsp baking powder
3 ml salt
25 ml butter
150 ml buttermilk
750 ml sunflower oil

Koeksisters can successfully be frozen for up to a month, and defrost within a few minutes.

METHOD

• To prepare the syrup, place all the syrup ingredients in a pot. Heat slowly and stir continuously until the sugar dissolves. Place the lid back on the pot and allow to simmer moderately for 1 minute. Remove the lid and simmer for another 5 minutes. Do not stir. Remove from the heat and allow to cool before refrigerating overnight.

• To prepare the dough, sift the flour, baking powder and salt together. Rub the butter into the mixture until it resembles fine breadcrumbs. Add the buttermilk and knead for 20 minutes until small air bubbles form. Cover with a damp cloth and allow to rest for 15 minutes.

• Roll the dough out to 3 mm and cut in rectangles of 8 x 3 cm. Cut each rectangle lengthways into 3 strips, taking care not to cut all the way down – in other words, the 'strips' should still be connected on one end. Plait each 3 times, and pinch the dough together after the last plait.

• Heat the oil and test whether it is hot enough by dropping a small piece of dough into the oil – the dough should bubble and gradually turn golden brown. Drop 2 koek-sisters at a time into the oil and flip them over to ensure that they are evenly golden brown in colour.

• Remove from the oil using a slotted spoon and place on paper towel for a few seconds and then immerse the hot koeksisters immediately in the ice-cold syrup.

• Place on cooling rack to cool and for the excess syrup to drain. Turn periodically.

madumbi fries

Serves 4

INGREDIENTS
4 large madumbis, peeled and cut into thin chip shapes
olive oil
Maldon sea salt

METHOD
• Preheat the oven to 180° C.
• Place the madumbis on an oven tray and toss them in oil. Then sprinkle with the sea salt and place in the oven.
• As soon as they turn a rich golden brown and they are cooked through, remove from the oven and serve as an accompaniment to a braai chop and a salad.

melkkos

Serves 6 to 8

INGREDIENTS
3 extra-large eggs
½ tsp salt
2 cups cake flour
water
2 litres milk
2 sticks cinnamon
cinnamon sugar

METHOD
• Gently beat the eggs and salt together. Add the cake flour and mix well. Add just enough water to form a stiff dough. Knead well until smooth and elastic. Roll out on a lightly floured surface to a thickness of 5 mm. Cut out thin strips of 4 to 5 mm thick. Toss the strips in cake flour.
• Pour the milk into a pot and add the cinnamon sticks. Bring to the boil. As soon as it begins to boil, add the strips of dough in small batches, stirring continually, until it has all been stirred into the milk.
• Bring to the boil again, reduce the heat and simmer for 15 to 25 minutes until the strips are cooked through and a fairly thick, milky porridge has formed.
• To serve, spoon into deep bowls and sprinkle with cinnamon sugar.

To make cinnamon sugar, simply mix white sugar with ground cinnamon.

mussel-and-litchi curry

INGREDIENTS

1 kg mussels
2 cups water
1 cup good-quality dry white wine

Curry sauce
4 tbsp olive oil
1 medium-sized onion, peeled and sliced
2 cloves garlic, peeled and crushed
2 tbsp medium-strength curry powder
1 ripe tomato, peeled and chopped
200 ml coconut milk
10 litchis, pips removed (or canned litchis)
45 ml dry sherry
salt and freshly milled black pepper to season

METHOD

• Rinse the mussels and place in a pot to which both the water and the wine have been added. Steam until the shells open. As soon as they have opened, remove from the heat and allow to cool. Clean the mussels by pinching the two sides of the shell together and pulling the 'beard' out. Set aside.

• To prepare the curry sauce, heat the oil in a saucepan and fry the onion until transparent. Turn the heat to low and add the garlic and fry until transparent. Add the curry powder and allow the heat to develop the flavours. Then add the tomato. Cook for 5 minutes on low heat.

• Pour the coconut milk over the curry mixture and allow to simmer for another 5 minutes. Add the litchis and the sherry and season. Cook for a further 10 minutes on a low heat. Remove from the heat.

• Add the mussels to the curry mixture and place the saucepan back on a low heat. Simmer for 5 to 10 minutes to give the flavours a chance to mingle.

• Serve with basmati rice and a pineapple salsa.

pineapple beer

Makes 5 litres

METHOD

- Add the grated pineapple to the water in a deep pot.
- Add the sugar and ginger to the mixture, and stir for 1 minute to combine all the ingredients.
- Cover and allow to stand for at least 24 hours, even more, at room temperature to allow it to ferment.
- Pour the mixture through a muslin cloth and into glass bottles. Keep refrigerated and serve cold.

INGREDIENTS

1 pineapple, peeled and coarsely grated
4½ litres water
1.2 kg sugar
1 tbsp ground ginger

In the cooler months, cover the pot with a small blanket and allow the mixture to stand in the warmest spot. It might take longer to ferment. Fermentation will cause bubbling on the surface of the drink.

pot-roasted Karoo lamb

Serves 4 to 6

INGREDIENTS

1 shoulder of lamb (± 3 kg)
olive oil
2 large red onions, peeled and
quartered
4 sun-dried tomatoes in olive oil
2 large cloves garlic, peeled
4 large carrots, peeled and cut into
chunks
1 bay leaf
salt and freshly milled black pepper
to taste
1 litre lamb stock
1 tbsp preserved lemons, finely
chopped

METHOD

• Place the shoulder of lamb in a large cast cast-iron pot.
• Drizzle with olive oil and add the onions. Brown the meat on both sides.
• Drain the sun-dried tomatoes and add them, together with the garlic, carrot chunks and bay leaf to the pot, and season with salt and pepper. Pour the stock into the pot and bring to the boil. Lower the heat and allow to simmer for 2 hours. Then add the preserved lemons and turn the heat up to allow the gravy to thicken.
• Serve on a bed of couscous.

roasted guinea fowl

Serves 4

METHOD

• Mix all the ingredients for the marinade together. Place the bird in the mixture and marinate overnight, with the breast covered in the juice.

• Preheat the oven to 180° C.

• Remove the bird from the marinade and pat dry. Season with salt and pepper and then drape the streaky bacon over the breast part, overlapping as far as possible.

• Place the guinea fowl, with breast and bacon facing upward, in an oven-proof dish and pour the marinade mixture over. Place into the oven and roast for 1½ hours.

• Carve the breast meat very thinly and serve the thighs and drumsticks – the rest of the bird has very little meat – on a bed of mashed potatoes with seasonal vegetables or a salad.

INGREDIENTS

Marinade

1 large carrot, peeled and cut into chunks
2 whole allspice
500 ml mango juice
1 leek, cleaned and cut into thick slices
2 bay leaves
1 guinea fowl

Roast

salt and freshly milled black pepper to season
200 g streaky bacon

When cooked, the meat of a guinea fowl is very dry because there is very little fat on the bird. Furthermore, the skin is tough, so if faced with the dilemma of preparing a guinea fowl for the pot, the easiest is to make a slit in the skin at the breast bone, and literally pull the skin off along with the feathers.

roti

Makes about 12

METHOD

• Mix the flour and salt in a mixing bowl. Use your fingertips to rub the oil into the flour mixture, until it resembles fine breadcrumbs. Add water to the mixture and mix to form a fairly soft dough.

• Roll the dough out on a floured surface to form a rectangle of about 20 x 35 cm in size. Use a palette knife to spread the softened butter onto the surface of the dough. Roll it up like a Swiss roll, cover with a tea towel and set aside for 30 minutes.

• Break off pieces the size of a tennis ball and form balls. Then roll these out to form discs the size of a fish plate. Fry in a hot skillet on one side until bubbles begin to form, then flip over to cook the other side. They should cook for about 2 minutes on each side.

INGREDIENTS

400 g all-purpose flour
1 tsp salt
3 tbsp oil
enough water to form soft, bread-like dough
1 cup soft butter

No oil should be necessary for frying because the dough already contains both butter and oil.

Rotis are a great accompaniment to any curry dish.

skaap stertjies

Serves 4

INGREDIENTS
8 sheep's tails, excess fat trimmed
8 medium-sized potatoes, peeled and halved lengthways
generous drizzle of olive oil
coarse salt and white pepper to season

METHOD
• Preheat the oven to 180° C.
• Place the sheep's tails and potatoes in a roasting pan, toss in the olive oil and sprinkle with the salt and pepper. Place in the oven and roast for an hour until golden brown and the potatoes are cooked through.
• Serve with seasonal vegetables or a tossed salad.

'Skaap stertjies' is Afrikaans for sheep tails.

smoked trout mini roulades

INGREDIENTS
100 g plain cream cheese
juice and finely grated zest of 1
lemon
200 g cold smoked trout ribbons
freshly ground black pepper

METHOD
• Mix the cream cheese, lemon juice and zest together in a bowl.
• Lay a sheet of plastic wrap flat on the working surface. Place the smoked trout ribbons, overlapping slightly, in a rectangle of about 10 cm wide, towards the bottom of the plastic wrap.
• Gently spread the cream cheese filling over the trout.
• To form the roulade, use the plastic wrap to fold one third of the width of the trout over to cover the middle third. Then peel the plastic away from the double layer of trout. Complete the process by using the far side of the plastic wrap to fold the remaining third of the trout layer on top of the first two thirds, forming a sausage shape. Now use the plastic to squeeze the three layers together into a tight roll. Refrigerate for 1 hour.
• Unwrap the trout roll and, using a very sharp knife, cut the 'sausage' shape into wheels of about 2 cm thick. Dip the tops into black pepper and serve as snacks before a meal.

This roll can be prepared a day in advance and kept in the refrigerator.

Lovely served as a starter with rocket and avo

soetkoekies

Makes 11 dozen

METHOD

- Preheat the oven to 200° C.
- Sift the flour, cream of tartar, bicarbonate of soda, salt and all the spices together. Add the sugar and mix well. Use your fingertips to rub the butter into the mixture until it resembles breadcrumbs. Add the eggs and the brandy and mix to form a stiff dough.
- On a lightly floured surface, roll the dough out to a thickness of about 3 mm. Cut out forms using a cookie cutter.
- Bake for 10 to 13 minutes until light golden brown.
- Cool on a rack and store in an airtight container.

INGREDIENTS

3 cups cake flour
½ tsp cream of tartar
½ tsp bicarbonate of soda
½ tsp salt
¼ tsp ground cloves
½ tsp five spice
½ tsp ground cinnamon
1¼ cup sugar
250 g butter
2 eggs, lightly beaten
2½ tsp brandy

Soetkoekies can be translated as 'sweet biscuits'.

sousboontjies

INGREDIENTS

500 g dried red speckled beans
water (to soak and cook the
beans)
4 tbsp sugar
100 ml vinegar
3 tbsp butter
1 tsp rosemary, very finely
chopped
2 tsp salt
white pepper to taste

METHOD

• Soak the beans in cold water overnight. Drain and place in a pot. Cover with fresh water and bring to boiling point. Cook for about 2 hours on a low heat until most of the water is absorbed and the beans are soft.
• Lightly mash some of them and add the rest of the ingredients. Season with the salt and pepper.
• Store in airtight containers.
• Serve cold with a braai.

waterblommetjie soup

INGREDIENTS

3 tbsp olive oil
1 tbsp butter
1 medium-sized onion, peeled and sliced
500 g fresh waterblommetjies
1 litre vegetable stock
salt and freshly milled black pepper to season
juice and fine zest of 1 lemon
125 ml fresh cream

METHOD

• Heat the oil in a pot. When hot, lower the heat a little and add the butter. As soon as the butter has melted, add the onion and fry until the onion begins to caramelise.

• Fry the waterblommetjies with the onion for 3 minutes. Add the stock and season with salt and pepper. Bring to a slow simmer and cook until tender.

• Using a hand blender, blend until smooth. Add the lemon juice and cream and bring to a slow simmer for 10 minutes.

• Just before serving, add the finely grated lemon zest.

Traditionally, waterblommetjies are served with suurings, wild Cape sorrel or *Oxalis pes-caprae*.

Suuring flowers are bright yellow and add a splash of colour to this dish.

Acknowledgements

The following were a great help and inspiration in writing this book:
Renata Coetzee, *The South African Culinary Tradition* (C. Struik, 1977)
Renata Coetzee, *Funa: Food from Africa* (Butterworth, 1982)
SJA de Villiers, *Kook en Geniet* (SJA de Villiers, 1975)
Hildagonda Duckitt, *Where is it?* (Chapman & Hall, 1925)
C Louis Leipoldt, *Leipoldt's Food and Wine* (Tafelberg, 1952)
Erica Platter, *East Coast Tables* (East Coast Radio, 2010)
Lannice Snyman, *Rainbow Cuisine* (Lannice Snyman Publishers, 1998)
Dine van Zyl, *Boerekos* (Human & Rousseau, 1985)
Southern African Sustainable Seafood Initiative (SASSI)
WWF
Statistics South Africa
The Department of Agriculture

Special thanks to:
Paddy Lindop
Laetitia Gerber
Tinus Lamprecht
Debbie Wieland
Nico Traut
Dawid Rossouw
Sean and Tracey Fraser of PHRASEworks
Jacana Media
Neil Austen

Photography:
Sophia Lindop, with contributions from Tinus Lamprecht: pp. 3, 6–7, 14, 17, 20, 24, 34, 62, 67, 71, 87, 88, 89, 101, 103, 105, 106; Debbie Wieland: pp. 10–11, 18–19, 25, 29, 37, 39, 46–47, 49, 51, 52, 68, 72, 82, 86, 97; Liesel Kershoff: pp. 8–9, 22, 41, 59, 61, 90; Gale McAll: pp. 4–5, 33, 44; Nico Traut: pp. 85, 98; Dawid Rossouw: p. 40; Morgenster: pp. 26

First published by Jacana Media (Pty Ltd in 2015

10 Orange Street
Sunnyside
Auckland Park 2092
South Africa
(+27 11) 628-3200
www.jacana.co.za

Print: 978-1-4314-2199-2
d-PDF: 978-1-4314-2200-5

Edited by Sean Fraser
Design and layout by Tracey Fraser
Set in Helvetica 9 pt
Job no. 002514
Printed and bound by Craft Print International Ltd

See a complete list of Jacana titles at www.jacana.co.za